MIND COACH

How to Teach Kids and Teenagers to Think Positive and Feel Good

Daniel G. Amen, M.D. Psychiatrist

Ant and Anteater Illustrations by James Hammock

© 2002 Mindworks Press

To Antony
You are what you think!

Introduction

Everything starts and ends in your mind. How your mind works determines how happy you are, how successful you feel and how well you interact with other people. The patterns of your mind encourage you toward greatness or they cause you to flounder in mediocrity or worse. Learning how to focus and direct your mind is the most important ingredient of success.

MIND COACH is a tool for parents on teaching children "thinking skills" that will help them be more effective in their day-to-day lives. Parents will also note that these skills will help them feel better and think in ways that help their interactions with their children.

MIND COACH is meant to be worked on together by parents and children. You may wish to read the book several times to solidify the material. Don't just let this sit on the shelf. MIND COACH has the potential to change the lives of children and teenagers if they use the principles in their day-to-day lives.

Thoughts That Hold You Back

"There's nothing to do."

"They always get to do everything and I don't get to do anything."

"No one ever plays with me."

"Anybody could have done that. I'm not so special."

"The teacher doesn't like me."

"The whole class will laugh at me."

"You don't love me."

"It's my fault they're getting a divorce."

"I'm so stupid."

"She didn't play with me today, she doesn't want to be my friend anymore."

"It's the teacher's fault."

These are examples of thoughts that severely limit a child's or teenager's ability to enjoy his or her life. How children think "moment by moment" has a huge impact on how they feel and how they behave. Negative thoughts often drive difficult behaviors and they cause most of the internal "feeling" problems that kids have, as well as the external or social problems. Hopeful thoughts, on the other hand, influence positive behaviors and lead children and teenagers to feel good about themselves and be more effective in their day-to-day lives.

Most difficult children and teenagers have a lot of negative thoughts. These thoughts come from many sources. Some of the negative thoughts come from what other people have told them about themselves (i.e., "You're no good! Why can't you ever mind? What's the matter with you. You make me crazy!"). Other negative thoughts originate from experiences where the child is continually frustrated, either at home or at school. They begin to think thoughts such as, "I'm stupid. I can't ever do anything right. It will never work out for me."

Your Brain Works Like a Computer

In many ways our brain works like a computer. When children receive negative **input** about themselves, they **store** it in their subconscious mind and they often **express** those messages in their negative behavior or feelings. Unless children are taught how to talk back to these harmful messages, they believe them 100%. This is a very important point. Most children (and adults) never challenge the thoughts that go through their head. They never even think about their own thoughts. They just believe what they think, even though the thoughts may be very irrational. This leads to behavior that is based on false ideas or false assumptions.

Positive Programming Versus Negative Programming

Parents, teachers and others often program the thoughts of children by how they talk to them. In dealing with children, it's important to program their mind with positive, uplifting, hopeful words, rather than critical or harsh words. This is especially true for children under six years old.

Many children have trouble thinking logically, because of their age (although this seems to be a common adult problem as well). Unfortunately, many children carry these negative thought patterns into adulthood, causing them to have problems with their moods and behavior.

These negative thoughts affect their moods and in many children become the seeds of anxiety or depression later on in life. It's critical to teach children about their thoughts and to teach them to challenge what they think, rather than just accepting thoughts blindly.

Teaching Children and Teenagers Thinking Skills

Unfortunately, when you're a child no one teaches you to think much about your thoughts or to challenge the notions that go through your head, even though your thoughts are always with you. Why do we spend so much time teaching kids about diagramming sentences and so little time teaching them how to think clearly? Most people do not understand how important thoughts are, and leave the development of thought patterns to random chance.

Did you know that thoughts have actual weight and mass? They are real! They have significant influence on every cell in your body (more detail on this in a little bit). When a child's mind is burdened with many negative thoughts, it affects their ability to learn, their ability to relate to other people and their physical health. Teaching kids how to control and direct their thoughts in a positive way will be one of the greatest gifts that anyone can give them.

Here are the actual step-by-step "positive thinking" principles that I use in my psychotherapy practice with children and teenagers. When children learn these principles, they gain more control over their feelings and their behavior. These principles will also significantly help parents as well.

STEP #1

Did you know...Every time you have a thought your brain releases chemicals. That's how our brain works.

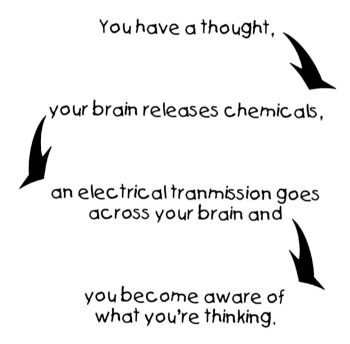

Thoughts are real and they have a real impact on how you feel and how you behave.

STEP #2

Every time you have a mad thought, an unkind thought, a sad thought, or a cranky thought, your brain releases negative chemicals that make your body feel bad. Whenever you're upset, imagine that your brain releases bubbles with sad or angry faces, looking to cause problems. Think about the last time you were mad. What feelings did you have inside your body? When most kids are mad, their muscles get tense, their heart beats faster, their hands start to sweat and they may even begin to feel a little dizzy. Your body reacts to every negative thought you have.

STEP #3

Every time you have a good thought, a happy thought, a hopeful thought or a kind thought your brain releases chemicals that make your body feel good. Whenever you have happy thoughts, imagine that your brain releases bubbles with glad or smiling faces, making you feel good. Think about the last time you had a really happy thought (such as when you got a good grade on a test or played with your pet). What feelings did you have inside your body? When most kids are happy, their muscles relax, their heart beats slower, their hands become dry and they breathe slower. Your body also reacts to your good thoughts.

STEP #4

Your body reacts to every thought you have. We know this from polygraphs or lie detector tests. During a lie detector test, you are hooked up to some very fancy equipment which measures:

hand temperature
heart rate
blood pressure
breathing rate
muscle tension and
how much the hands sweat

The tester then asks you questions, like "Did you do that thing?" If you did the bad thing, your body is likely to have a **"stress response"** and it is likely to react in the following ways:

hands get colder
heart goes faster
blood pressure goes up
breathing gets faster
muscles get tight and
hands sweat more

Almost immediately, your body reacts to what you think, whether you say anything or not. Now the opposite is also true. If you did not do the thing they are asking you about it is likely that your body will experience a **"relaxation response"** and react in the following ways:

hands will become warmer
heart rate will slow
blood pressure goes down
breathing becomes slower and deeper
muscles become more relaxed and
hands become drier

Again, almost immediately, your body reacts to what you think. This not only happens when you're asked about telling the truth, your body reacts to every thought you have, whether it is about school, friends, family or anything else.

STEP #5

Thoughts are very powerful. They can make your mind and your body feel good or they can make you feel bad. Every cell in your body is affected by every thought you have. That is why when people get emotionally upset, they actually develop physical symptoms, such as headaches or stomach aches. Some people even think that people who have a lot of negative thoughts are more likely to get cancer. If you can think about good things you will feel better.

Did you know that Abraham Lincoln (our 16th president) had periods of bad depression when he was a child and later as an adult? He even thought about killing himself and had some days when he didn't even get out of bed. In his later life, however, he learned to treat his bad feelings with laughter. He became a very good story-teller and loved to tell jokes. He learned that when he laughed, he felt better. Over a hundred years ago, people knew that thoughts were very important!

Abraham Lincoln knew the value of positive thoughts. He used laughter to treat depression.

STEP #6

Unless you think about your thoughts, they are **automatic or "they just happen."** Since they just happen, they are not always correct. Your thoughts do not always tell you the truth. Sometimes they even lie to you. I once knew a boy who thought he was stupid, because he didn't do well on tests. When we tested his IQ (intelligence level), however, we discovered that he was close to a genius! You don't have to believe every thought that goes through your head. It's important to think about your thoughts to see if they help you or they hurt you. Unfortunately, if you never challenge your thoughts, you just "believe them" as if they were true.

STEP #7

You can train your thoughts to be positive and hopeful, or you can just allow them to be negative and upset you. Once you learn about your thoughts you can chose to think good thoughts and feel good, or you can choose to think bad thoughts and feel lousy. That's right, it's up to you! You can learn how to change your thoughts and you can learn to change the way you feel.

One way to learn how to change your thoughts is to notice them when they are negative and talk back to them. If you can correct negative thoughts you take away their power over you. When you have a negative thought without challenging it, your mind believes it and your body reacts to it.

STEP #8

As I mentioned above, negative thoughts are mostly automatic. They "just happen." I call these bad thoughts "**A**utomatic **N**egative **T**houghts." If you take the first letter from each of these words it spells the word **ANT**.

Think of these negative thoughts that invade your mind like ants that bother people at a picnic. One negative thought, like one ant at a picnic, is not a big problem. Two or three negative thoughts, like two or three ants at a picnic, becomes more irritating. Ten or twenty negative thoughts, like ten or twenty ants at a picnic, can cause real problems.

Whenever you notice these automatic negative thoughts or ANTs, you need to crush them or they'll begin to ruin your whole day. One way to crush these ANTs is to write down the negative thought and talk back to it. For example, if you think, "Other kids will laugh at me when I give my speech" write it down and then write down a positive response; something like, "The other kids will like my speech and find it interesting." When you write down negative thoughts and talk back to them, you take away their power and help yourself feel better.

Some kids tell me they have trouble talking back to these negative thoughts because they feel that they are lying to themselves. Initially, they believe that the thoughts that go through their mind are true. Remember, thoughts sometimes lie to you. It's important to check them out before you just believe them!

ANTs: Automatic Negative Thoughts

Here are nine different ways that our thoughts lie to us to make situations out to be worse than they really are. Think of these nine ways as different species or types of ANTs (Automatic Negative Thoughts).
When you can identify the type of ANT, you begin to take away the power it has over you. I have labeled some of these ANTs as red, because these ANTs are particularly harmful to you. Notice and exterminate ANTs whenever possible.

Ant Species #1
All or Nothing Thinking

These thoughts happen when you make something out to be all good or all bad. There's nothing in between. You see everything in black or white terms. The thought, "There's nothing to do," is an example. When you say "There's nothing to do" you feel down and upset. You feel bored and unmotivated to change the situation. You just whine or complain. But is, "There's nothing to do" a rational thought? Of course not, it's just a thought. Even on a day when it's raining outside and you have to stay in, you can probably list 20 things to do if you put your mind to it: draw, make paper airplanes, write a story, read a story, do a puzzle, write grandma a letter, play hide and seek, do your chores (a novel thought), etc. But if you never challenge the thought, "There's nothing to do," then you just believe it and spend the rest of the day feeling crummy. Other examples of "all or nothing thinking" for kids include thoughts such as, "I'm the worst ballplayer in the city. If I get an 'A' on this test I'm a great student, but if I do poorly then I'm no good at all."

Ant Species #2
"Always" Thinking

This happens when you think something that happened will "always" repeat itself. For example, if your mother is irritable and she gets upset you might think to yourself, "She's always yelling at me." Even though she yells only once in a while. But just the thought "She's **always** yelling at me" is so negative that it makes you feel sad and upset. Whenever you think in words like **always, never, no one, everyone, every time, everything,** these are examples of "always" thinking and are usually wrong. There are many examples of "always" thinking: "They always get to do everything, and I don't get to do anything. No one ever plays with me. Everyone is always picking on me. You never take me swimming. You always get her what she wants." This type of ANT is very common. Watch out for it.

Ant Species #3
Focusing on the Negative

This occurs when your thoughts **only see the bad in a situation** and ignore any of the good parts. For example, if you have to move, even though you're sad to leave your friends, you don't think of the new places you'll see and the new friends you'll make. It's very important, if you want to keep your mind healthy, to focus on the good parts of your life a lot more than the bad parts.

I once helped a child who was depressed. In the beginning he could only think about the bad things that happened to him. He had recently move to my city and he told me that he would never have friends (even though he already had several), he would do poorly in his new school (even though he got mostly good grades) and that he would never have any fun (even though he lived near a bay and an amusement park). By focusing on the negative in his new situation, he was making it very hard on himself to adjust to his new home. He would have been much better off if he looked at all the positives in the situation rather than the negatives.

Negative children can learn a powerful lesson from the Disney movie "Pollyanna." In the movie, Pollyanna went to live with her aunt after her missionary parents had died. Even though she had lost her parents, she was able to help many "negative people" with her attitude. She introduced them to the "glad game," to look for things to be glad about in any situation. Her father had taught her this game after she had experienced a disappointment. She always wanted a doll, but her parents never had enough money to buy it for her. Her father sent a request for a secondhand doll to his missionary sponsors. By mistake, they sent her a pair of crutches. "What is there to be glad about crutches?" they thought. Then they decided they could be glad because they didn't have to use them. This very simple game changed the attitudes and lives of many people in the movie. The minister was especially affected by Pollyanna.

Before she came to town, he preached hell, fire and damnation, but he did not seem to be very happy. Pollyanna told him that her father said that the Bible had 800 "Glad Passages," and that if God mentioned being glad that many times, it must be because he wants us to think that way. Focusing on the negative will make you feel bad. Playing the glad game, or looking for the positive, will help you feel better.

Ant Species #4
Fortune Telling

This is where you **predict the worst possible outcome** of a situation. For example, before you have to give a speech in front of the class you might say to yourself, "Other kids will laugh at me and think I'm stupid." Just having this thought will make you feel nervous and upset. I call "fortune telling" red ANTs because they really hurt your chances for feeling good.

I once treated a 10-year-old boy, named Kevin, who stuttered in class whenever he read out loud. In private, he was a wonderful reader, but whenever he started to read in class he thought to himself, "I'm a lousy reader; the other kids will laugh at me." Because he had these thoughts, he stopped raising his hand to volunteer to read. In fact, this thought made him so upset that he started getting sick before school and missed nearly a month of school before his mother brought him to see me. He also stopped answering the telephone at home for fear that he would stutter whenever he said hello. When he told me about the thoughts he had in class and at home, I understood the problem. When you predict that bad things will happen, such as you will stutter, your mind then often makes them happen. For this child, when he imagined himself stuttering, he then stuttered whenever he read in class.

The treatment for Kevin was to get him to replace those negative thoughts and pictures in his head with the image of him being a wonderful reader in class. I also taught him to breathe slowly when he read and to think good thoughts. I also made him the designated person to answer the telephone at home. Whenever you're afraid of unreasonable things (such as answering the telephone or reading in class), it is important to face your fears. Otherwise, fears develop power over you. Over the next couple of weeks he was able to go back to school, and he even volunteered to read. At home, his mother told me that he ran to answer the telephone whenever it rang. If you are going to predict anything at all, it is best to predict the best. It will help you feel good and it will help your mind make it happen.

Ant Species #5
Mind Reading

This happens when you believe that you know what another person is thinking when they haven't even told you. Many people mind read, and it often gets them into trouble. It is one of the major reasons kids have trouble with their friends. I tell kids, "Please don't read anybody's mind; they have enough trouble reading it themselves!" You know that you are mind reading when you have thoughts such as, "Those kids are mad at me. You don't like me. They were talking about me."

I once treated a teenager, Dave, who had this problem so badly that he would hide in clothes racks at the shopping mall so that other kids wouldn't see him. He told me, "If they see me, they'll think I look funny and then they'll want to tease me." He became very nervous around other people because he worried about what others thought of him. He finally realized that other teenagers were more worried about themselves and they really spent little time thinking about him. Avoid reading anyone's mind. You never know what they are thinking.

Ant Species #6
Thinking With Your Feelings

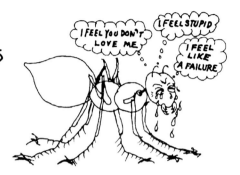

This occurs when you believe your negative feelings without ever questioning them. Feelings are very complex, and, as I mentioned above, feelings sometimes lie to you. But many people believe their feelings even though they have no evidence for them. "Thinking with your feelings" thoughts usually start with the words "I feel." For example, "I feel like you don't love me. I feel stupid. I feel like a failure. I feel nobody will ever trust me." Whenever you have a strong negative feeling, check it out. Look for the evidence behind the feeling. Do you have real reasons to feel that way? Or, are your feelings based on events or things from the past?

Here's an example. Matt, age 10, had a problem learning. He also got expelled from his school for fighting. He felt that he was stupid and that he was a bad boy. When I first met him I knew that he had a problem called Attention Deficit Disorder which I could help him fix with the right medication. He started the medicine and went to a new school. He did wonderful! He did so well, in fact, that his old school (which was a better school) was willing to take him back. When his mother told him this good news, he became very upset. He said that he felt that he would fail and have lots of problems. He was letting the "old" feelings from the past mess up his chance for a new start. When he corrected his negative feelings by talking back to them, he was able to return to his old school. He even made the honor roll!

Ant Species #7
Guilt Beatings

Guilt is not a helpful emotion, even for kids. In fact, guilt often causes you to do those things that you don't want to do. Guilt beatings happen when you think in words like "should, must, ought or have to." Here are some examples: "I should be nice to my younger brother. I must never lie. I ought to call my grandmother. I have to do my homework." Because of human nature, whenever we think that we "must" do something, no matter what it is, we don't want to do it.

Remember the story of Adam and Eve. The only restriction that God put on them when he gave them the Garden of Eden was that they shouldn't eat from the Tree of Knowledge. Almost immediately after God told them what they "shouldn't do" they started to wonder why they shouldn't do it. Well, you know the rest of the story. They ate from the tree and ended up being kicked out of the Garden of Eden. It is better to replace "guilt beatings" with phrases like "I want to do this... It fits my goal to do that... It would be helpful to do this..." So in our examples above, it would be helpful to change those phrases to "I want to be nice to my younger brother. It's helpful for me not to lie, because people will trust me. I want to call my grandmother. It's in my best interest to do my homework."

Ant Species #8
Labeling

Whenever you attach a negative label to yourself or to someone else, you impair your ability to take a clear look at the situation. Some examples of negative labels that kids use are "nerd," "jerk," "idiot," "spoiled brat" and "clown." Negative labels are very harmful, because whenever you call yourself or someone else a spoiled brat or an idiot you lump that person in your mind with all of the "spoiled brats" or "idiots" that you've ever known and you become unable to deal with them in a reasonable way. Stay away from negative labels.

Ant Species #9
Blame

You can ruin your life if you have a strong tendency to blame other people when things go wrong, if you take no responsibility for your problems. When something goes wrong at home or at school, people who use blame thinking try to find someone to blame. They rarely admit their own problems. Typically, you'll hear statements from them like:

"It wasn't my fault that..."

"That wouldn't have happened if you had..."

"How was I supposed to know..."

"It's your fault that..."

The bottom line statement goes something like this: "If only you had done something differently then I wouldn't be in the predicament I'm in. It's your fault, and I'm not responsible."

Now, blaming others starts early. I have three children. When my youngest, Katie, was 18 months old, she would blame her brother, who was 11, for any trouble she might be in. Her nickname for him was Didi, and "Didi did it," even if he wasn't home. One day she spilled a drink at the table while her mother's back was turned. When her mother turned around and saw the mess she asked what had happened. Katie told her "Didi spilled my drink." When her mother told her that her brother was at a friend's house, Katie persisted, "Didi did it. He came home, spilled my drink and then he left."

Whenever you blame someone else for the problems in your life you become powerless to change anything. Many kids play the "Blame Game," but it rarely helps them. Stay away from blaming thoughts and take personal responsibility to change the problem you have.

SUMMARY OF ANT SPECIES:
(Automatic Negative Thoughts)

 1. All or Nothing Thinking: thoughts that are all good or all bad.

 2. "Always" Thinking: thinking in words like always, never, no one, everyone, every time, everything.

 3. Focusing on the Negative: only seeing the bad in a situation.

 4. Fortune Telling: predicting the worst possible outcome of a situation.

 5. Mind Reading: believing that you know what another person is thinking even though they haven't told you.

6. Thinking With Your Feelings: believing negative feelings without ever questioning them.

 7. Guilt Beatings: thinking in words like "should, must, ought or have to."

 8. Labeling: attaching a negative label to yourself or to someone else.

 9. Blame: blaming someone else for the problems you have.

KILLING THE ANTs
(Talking Back To Negative Thoughts)

Whenever you notice an ANT entering your mind, train yourself to get rid of it. In a sense you become an exterminator of bad thoughts. To do this, write down the automatic negative thoughts (ANTs) that go through your mind. Then identify their species (such as "always thinking" or "mind reading"). Finally, kill the ANT by talking back to the irrational thought. When you do this exercise, you begin to take away the power of the ANTs and gain control over how you feel. Here are several examples from some of the bad thoughts at the beginning of the book.

ANT	SPECIES	KILL THE ANT
There's nothing to do.	All or Nothing Thinking	There are probably lots of things to do if I think about it for awhile.
No one ever plays with me.	Always Thinking	That's silly. I have played with a lot of kids.
The teacher doesn't like me.	Mind Reading	I don't know that. Maybe she's just having a bad day.
The whole class will laugh at me.	Fortune Telling	I don't know that. Maybe they'll really like my speech.
I'm stupid.	Labeling	Sometimes I do things that aren't that smart, but I'm not stupid!
It's the teacher's fault.	Blame	I need to look at my part of the problem and look for ways I can make the situation better.

Your thoughts matter! Train them to be positive and it will help your mind, your body and your relationships.